Golden Stars

reclaiming you

Written by:

Alana Lima Johnson

Book cover designed by:

Ravi Lima

Golden Stars

Golden Stars

For anyone in
the journey of
reclaiming
themselves
after:

heartbreak

rejection

change

people pleasing

losing yourself

grief

judgement

Golden Stars

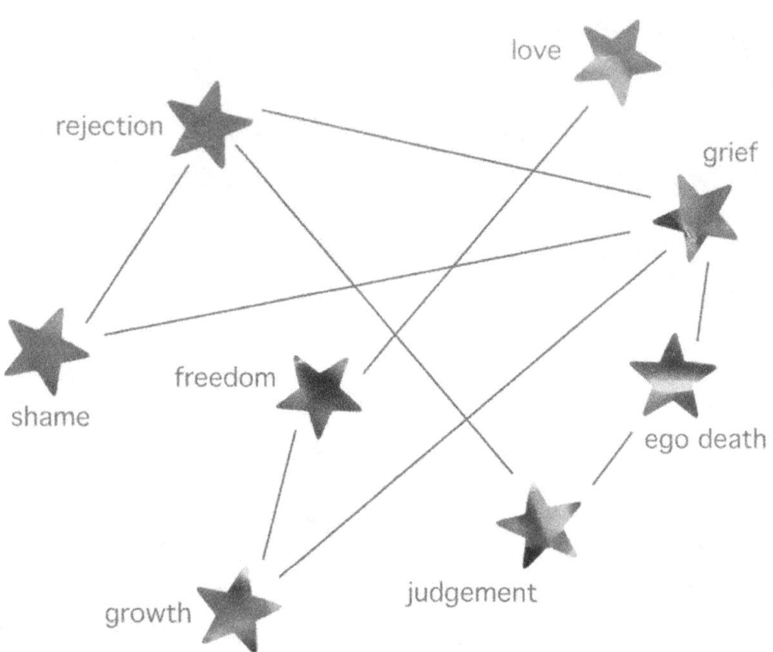

sometimes the only way forward is through

Table of Contents

coming undone.

Golden Stars

we don't marvel at the stars at noon
even though they are as present as they are at midnight
the sun outshines them and we forget about their existence

that's the beautiful thing about contrast
thc darkness enhances the light
and we're able to appreciate the blessings more
like when we gaze at the stars at night

I let you crucify me
silence me
I let myself believe
your pain was greater
and so I let you use me as a shield
how silly of me
to believe I was made of steel
the paper armor I wore
was shredded to pieces on the floor
you took pleasure in
feeding
your skewed narrative to
the hungry dogs
and eventually
my truth
the stories
that I kept private
to protect you from seeming flawed
held no more importance in the bottom of the ocean
and neither did my voice

how could I ever compete with the mountainous waves you created at the surface?

I wanted you to pick me like you do your
favorite food on the menu

you rejected me like sour milk instead it
hurt
and for a moment
I too believed I was rotten

I wear her like a cloak
no one can see her
but I am reminded of her every time I go out
I feel her weight on my shoulders

sometimes I wish she had magical
powers to make me invisible too
if only it was possible
I wear her like a cloak
but she feels like a tattoo

somehow finding a way to blend into my skin
at moments I don't know where I end
and she begins

I wear her like a cloak
not intentionally I suppose
I just can't seem to shake her off
because every time I look at someone else's
eyes I can see her in my reflection

she's always finding a way
to remind me she is here to stay

-shame

Golden Stars

I couldn't hide her
like I did alone in my room with grief and anger
shame was visible from every angle
she wasn't much of a stay-in type of gal
she followed me every time I left the house
I ignored her
she crinkled my clothes with her grip
I wanted to bury her
but the more I forced her to leave
the stronger she grasped onto me

I am made up of broken pieces
scattered on the floor like a porcelain doll
each piece written with a sharpie
words off my screen

the ones you typed in one second
now ingrained in my skin

the ink sunk so deep
my blood turned black

my heart stopped for a moment
it shattered me apart

I stood in a dark room
lit dimly by a waning moon
looking at myself on the ground
wondering if there will be a day
that I'll have the strength to put the pieces back in place

If so
I fear
I'll never be the same

they say disappointment
blooms from the seeds of expectations
no wonder I have disappointed many
I'm not a rose or a daisy
I'm a wildflower
an improv song
if you choose to tag along
don't expect me to be red or yellow
don't expect me to have the softest petals
because maybe I will satisfy your idea of me
but most likely I won't
I change as I grow
unpredictable and bold
I don't really fit in with comfort
I'm more of going with the flow
finding peace in the chaos of the ocean
I don't resist the tides
and if it's too much to hold me during the wind
I don't expect you to stay
you can rest inside
I'm happy solo dancing
in the rain

— so don't get too attached to a version of me —

my heart was made of glass
I wrapped it in velvet sheets
it was fragile
it was so beautiful to see
I wore it on display
I guess that lured you in
you manipulated every security code
to tear it through my clothes

the fragility of my heart
reflected that of my self-love
when you dropped it on the ground
it splattered on the floor

when I finally had the space
I mended my heart back in place
except I used rubber instead of glass
now my heart loves through the pain

Golden Stars

I walk around in the grocery store
smile on my way out
no one in there would have known
I am aching inside
no Advil can alleviate
the pain of my invisible wounds
I have no excuse to stay back alone in my room
if I had a broken bone it would all be so different
I would be dedicating 99% of my time to heal
instead here I am
walking around town
pretending my heart is made of steel

my door frame is swollen
there's a monsoon on the other side
I've been holding on
wearing a smile and some shades
scared you could see through my broken gaze
it's only a matter of time
until my laughter turns into a silent cry
it takes one tear to draw in the rain

the forecast doesn't look great
I'll probably be staying in
moving through my pain

it's hard to look you in the eyes
I'm too scared I'll see through your gaze
feel your perception of me slip for a moment
between one blink
and for a second I will think
what you perceive is real
I'll cringe at the thought of being seen through
your tainted rumored lenses
I will want to bury my face beneath my feet
as my mouth keeps entertaining your small talk
but before you know it
I'll find any excuse to walk
away and wish
I never looked up
to meet your gaze

I don't go out much these days

wrongful conviction is egos
greatest fear
to be judged for something you're
not
the inner need to defend your
image
the injustice pulling at every inch of your skin
the shame that shouldn't be there in the first place
the disbelief that they actually think you are who
you're not
the urge to hide and protect your heart
your ego may try to prove who you are
but before you burn your own wick to its last flames
save your breath instead
breathe into your heart
space
no matter what they think of
you
remember your truth
has never
and
can't
ever be
swayed

every cell in my body feels corrupted this
veil that covers me
makes it hard to breathe

I try to swim to the surface
but their words are like quicksand holding me
just beneath

close enough for me to reach for
the light
and yet feel trapped in the dark

you'll dance with me where shadows are casted
but you're shy of the sun
or I should say
you won't go out with me on a sunny day
you prefer the dimly lit places
when we're together
where I blend in with the scene
where whispers can't travel with the wind

how *dare* you be seen with me

but your words would never reveal
the manipulation behind your intentions

you love me in secrecy

and honestly
I rather you not love me at all
than to love me secretly

they liked the way I made them feel
in the same way we like the feeling of
sunshine on our skin
in the selfish way we complain when the sky is gray
or when the rays are too bright for our eyes to rest
opened

they liked me the same way we like the sun

only when its in the perfect place
at the perfect time

and when it rains

they don't miss me
they miss the sunshine

one of the hardest truths to digest:
some of the closest people to you
are praying for your downfall

when you reach your hand up
expecting them to care
they don't seem to be there at all

instead they leave you

turn their heads
celebrating your defeat
behind your back

they judge while they carry dirt
on their holy hands

make it
make sense

they say it's important to let people go
"some people you'll naturally outgrow"

but it hurts to lose old friends

a part of your childhood is tainted on their way out
memories that can't ever be replayed the same

moments that were so colorful now feel *gray*

one moment we were friends
then one day we exchanged our final text
neither of us knew it would be the last
message you would send and I would reply
and then neither of us would try
to hold on any longer
we were drifting and
it was about time we stopped resisting
life was doing its thing
taking people to places
our journeys no longer involved each other
we took different exits
and the distance was only growing longer
but I like to think for a brief moment
that our paths merged
our souls had the opportunity to learn
sending us both on our separate ways
with a little extra wisdom and love

for a while I didn't have the energy to make new
friends
I kept making excuses that I was in a different season
in my life
focusing on myself or my career and that I didn't need
new friends at least not yet
I think it's all partially true but really if I were to be
honest
it's not that I'm too busy
it's that my heart is still healing from the friendships
that failed
I still try to make sense of them to no avail
some people just grow apart
friendship breakups are weird
and you're just expected to move on
except my heart kind of still breaks
thinking that one day I'll tell my kids the stories of
when we were young
and I'll bring up your name
and they'll ask me "who is that mom?"
to which I will reply "oh just someone from my past"

how did you become just *that*?

after all these years
I thought you'd know me better

yet it only took one rumor
for you to doubt my character

they say dark times
will reveal to you
who’s a true friend

I don’t know
what hurt more

the dark times
or to witness
our friendship
come to an end

I learned the difference between alone and lonely
lonely doesn't necessarily mean you are alone
lonely is more of a feeling of not belonging
a longing for someone who also understands
who sees life from a similar lens
actually the times you feel most lonely
are those when you're surrounded by people
who don't feel like home
in contrast you don't necessarily need to feel lonely
when you are alone

I used to divide myself into portions
lay them on the menu with assorted flavors
to please all the different people
that came to the table

until I realized to no surprise
people pleasing was an impossible task
they kept trying to divide me even further in half

I was merely a sampler for everyone
to taste
judge
and forget

-people pleasing

it's hard not to get in my head
in a crowded room
I can't help but assume
every glance pointed my way
is heavy with opinion
there are consequences to living
so openly bold
you expose yourself
to what feels like the world
people think they know you
but they actually don't

the hardest part was resisting the downfall
when I finally surrendered to the collapse

life started to do its thing
and before I knew it
it all made sense

even the bitter ends

they don't have to get it
you know?
why you did the thing
why you changed your mind
why you chose this path

you don't have to over-explain your heart
because odds are
they still won't get it

they were never supposed to
get it

the pressure is off

there is ice on the ground
your footsteps now covered by snow
winter has come to reset my aching soul
your traces will be washed away when spring is here
I'll bloom into a new version of me
the person I've craved to be
but I fear
the ice will freeze your marks on my skin instead
and even in the summer months
when I'm meant to expand into the horizon
part of me will still remain frozen with you in the past

Golden Stars

I can’t quite put my finger on when
or where I lost her
it must have been somewhere in between giving too
much and never feeling good enough
before I knew it
she faded into the background
I’ve been looking for her in old journals

I miss her
I should’ve never let her drift so far

we don't judge the trees for losing their leaves in fall
we praise the change and beauty
that marks a new season
so why are we so harsh with ourselves when
we are not shining like summer
or growing flowers like spring

fall and winter are beautiful too
aren't they?

I overthink
the worst part is
I don’t overthink the future
as much as I overthink the past

I can validate overthinking the future
say I’m playing life like a chess game
but I can’t explain or make sense of
overthinking something I can’t change

I can’t go back
I can’t replay
I must only accept if not regret
yet I still play this game in my head
“what if I had decided to take a different path?”

I'm not afraid of feeling
but I learned to fear the silence
my emotions reached the threshold of experience
triggering my brain to cut off the signal waves
and I went numb
just like a ringing in my ear right after a bomb

the ring
a sound that kept me awake
to experience it all
but there was no more pain
sounds nice?

but what is living if you don't feel alive?
my soul was silent
my expression was absent
the sun still set and rose on the same horizon
I clung to my flesh as if to beg
gravity to keep me somewhat grounded
I prayed for tears for the dam
I created to clear
could I just feel something?

I get on my knees
I ask for the very thing I once cursed

to be *human*

Golden Stars

it's not black and white
like the movies paint it to be
heroes and villains
one story
two sides
to hear and to experience
are two different things
how can you claim to know
if you weren't there behind the scenes?
there's duality and depth to perspective
if I tell you I am only the hero
simultaneously I reject any responsibility
the victim perhaps to my own reality
not to discredit victimhood
however the truth is I'm not the hero nor the villain
I am just a human
with faults
mistakes
but a heart of love
and forgiveness

if choosing myself
in the name of self-love
makes me the villain of your story
I rather die the villain than the martyr
that forever sacrificed to please your ideal reality

my ego won't let me get on my knees and pray
my ego whispers in my ear "everyone is looking get up"
my ego distances me from god

— dear ego I've had enough—

don't shy away from rejection
the lack of acceptance teaches you something
love would never know how to

like how it's more sustainable to cultivate your own garden
instead of getting lost trying to find
what you need at someone else's market

I swallow back my words
shove them down into my belly
no wonder I haven't been hungry

I'm too busy digesting the emotions I never spoke
they say bottling up is no way to cope

the longer I don't let go
the further I am from myself
I've been quiet for too long
wishing for it all to be gone
except this isn't a dream
it's reality
the only way to move on
is to let my emotions
roll off my tongue

the world loves strong women
yet they don't talk about how
little girls weren't born resilient

when life brought them down to their knees
when their heart breaks stripped away every last tear
from their face

when men made them feel less
and when the systems corrupted their minds
to believe their worth was tied
to trends that change like tides
they chose to rise

to be brave and pick up the pieces that were
never meant to break

and so next time you look in the eyes
of a strong woman
I hope you realize
her strength was not built overnight

death is as present as life is
at all times

how many versions of you have already died?

to know death
is to embrace being alive

if you walk in your truth
you will never fear missing
out on a life you dreamed of
but never
had the courage to live

on the days that it feels hard to sleep in your own skin
when you wish you had claws to pull your heart out of your chest
when your stomach demands to be cuddled up
on the days in which you question what is the point of life and feeling so much

I hope something or someone reminds you
that although there will be days
in which your heart breaks
into a million of pieces
there will also be a day
in which you'll feel ready to put them back in place

when I found myself standing in the ruins of my old life
I was practically alone with a few others who
stuck by my side
the old paradigm crumbled
and with it went old friends
labels
my old self

the ashes on the ground
made up of parts of me
I had to release
in order to have the strength to
breathe life into a new city
that awaited me

I find myself shedding layers
like clothes that no longer fit
thoughts that no longer serve
words that I no longer peak
the fear of letting go of the old
slowly detaching from my soul
a tree must shed its leaves to grow new ones
and so should we
I once thought life was about
gathering things
and having a full house
I now see fulfillment and a crowded space
don't always correlate
life has taught me too many times
if we wish to grow
we must let go

-making space for the next phase

when money was low
friends were few
path uncertain
and the future unknown
I finally felt like I was coming back home to my soul

when this material life
didn't provide satisfaction for my ego to thrive
I had to seek shelter inside

it was through my undoing
unbecoming and
deconditioning that I excavated the essence of my existence

Golden Stars

I was once told I was too loud
and so I began to swallow my words and not speak out
I was once told I was too dressed up
and so I began to wear less pink and no makeup
I was once told others would judge
and so I left my light on my nightstand every day I woke up
until one day
I was everything they wanted me to be and still not enough
even my reflection stared back at me in disgust
it took me looking at a stranger's eyes in the mirror
to realize
I never had to change
or dim my own light

"I want to be a good human"
at times that feels like an internal competition of
how far I will overextend
I'll put my flesh against the blade
of life so that you will smile one more time
when there is rain
I'll let you be the succulent and I'll be the desert
taste every drop of nectar
and leave me with your leftovers
"no really I insist"
I know
it's an exhausting
way to live
it's a silent sacrifice
always putting yourself second
and time will reveal
it is unsustainable
this whole martyr ordeal
but at that point
you have people to please
bending isn't an option
but rather an expectation to keep the peace
to choose yourself becomes an act of rebellion
you against your deep-rooted guilt
the heaviness of their inevitable disappointment
compressing your heart
"I am sorry I can't do this anymore"
is just good not enough

when they demand what you're no longer willing to give
you're painfully forced to learn that choosing you
is also a self-less act
your purpose was never to mold into everyone's dreams
neglecting your own
to be a good human doesn't
make it wrong
to prioritize yourself
but you have to be willing to watch
others feel distraught
at your audacity to put yourself first

nothing resonates anymore
I feel it once again
the clothes that once hugged my skin
making me crawl underneath
the urge to crumble everything
I've ever identified with into a paper ball
as I decondition
I don't relate with my work
with my inspiration
or my goals
nothing makes sense at all
yet the sun and the moon still rise
and the world around me still feels the same
but inside I don't see things in the same way
I don't know who I am
what I like or what I want to do with my life
I've learned that when I'm here
In these moments I like to call the
beautiful and chaotic *in between*
the harder I try to plan or figure it all out
the further I get from myself
and so I surrender
like I've done many times before
I allow it come
the clarity the eureka moment
that my soul oh so craves for

– what is next shall unfold in perfect timing

we build castles to tell stories of who we are
each stone a title our ego has claimed
walls made up with opinions we deemed true
concrete layers lathered by each person
that has something to validate about you
a castle might be tall
recognized by everyone
who walks by
yet what is the point of a sand castle
that is hollow inside?

a beautiful palace with locked doors
is no different than a prison

a bird can sing beautifully
but with cut-off wings
it will never feel free

you see
sometimes we build castles
we realize we don't want to live in

forever looking out the window
wondering how we became our own prisoner

it's easy to forget that
the chains created
can be destroyed
just as easily
turn those same stones
into dust
let the concrete
run like water
when you decide you no longer wish to stay
in the confinements of who you say you are.

because freedom and power aren't found amongst
the empty hallways of castles and palaces
they are found when you let your home be the forest
vines growing wild.

when messy becomes the perfect place
for you to play and change,
where there is no quicksand
holding you down to one version of you.

you are ever-evolving, ever-growing.
rebirthing with every breath.
A walking queen or king,
with a whole empire within.
never needed a concrete castle to begin with.

— find your power by breaking through the very walls
you created

pride is a glass that breaks at the brink of death
as you lay there on shattered glass
moments before you go
will you regret
protecting pride to satisfy a fragile ego?

the wrong choice
is the enemy of *love*

sometimes choices are hard
but what's harder is defying your heart

we tend to believe the mind stores memories
but the grasp of memories fade

unlike a feeling

the heart will never forget how it felt to break

Golden Stars

it takes one second to change your life
one decision
one text
one button pressed
It takes just one second

does that frighten you or excite you?
can you handle the tidal waves that come with change?
the silent sting from destruction and the ashes of the past?
can you handle that the right choices don't always feel pretty?
that the grass may be greener, and yet you may feel a bit gray in the process?

it takes one second
to change it all

I won't lie to you
you can't escape or skip the emotional hurricane that follows any big change

but as everything you knew crumbles
the seeds of doubt are fertilized
with opportunity

I hope when your flowers bloom
you recognize the beauty
in your courage to not only welcome change
but also to be the one
to choose it

mending the heart.

Alana Lima Johnson

The problem was
I thought
I was made of wood

not literally
but in the way
wood chips and breaks

and I used to believe people could chip me away
or I would
give pieces of myself

sometimes intentionally and other times
not necessarily

and I believed certain experiences would
leave marks and stains and
these would of course never go away

but regardless every year
I would try to polish it all away
sand it down
and inevitably it would make me more refined
and smaller
and I'd get so obsessed with making sure
the surface looked perfect

that sometimes I would overdo it
and I'd have to compensate

and the problem was never my ever-fading worth
the problem was that I thought I was made of wood

Golden Stars

the winter seasons in my life
have taught me how to love the places
in my soul where the sun forgot to touch

summer nights may rob hearts
but nothing feels as deep as sober love

for when it's cold you must be your own flame
and darling if you can spark in the winter
you'll light the world on fire in the summer rain

be your own sun and your light will never set
your blood won't run cold either
and even through the blizzards
your heart will be dripping with gold
for winters have taught you things summer couldn't
ever know

like how to grow flowers through the snow

be grateful for your perceived misfortunes

if you spend time focusing on the lack
you may just miss your fortunes

-a *lesson taught by my dad -*

Golden Stars

where there is change there is grief
it's okay to feel sad and excited all at once
because even what you let go of
can feel so familiar
in a way a part of you
that when you let go you feel the blues
it's ok to spend some time confused and perplexed at why
you feel so depressed when there is so much beauty that lies
ahead
in your path there will be pivots and turns
and some may sting a little deeper than others
your ego is stretching and sore
give it time to adjust to your new norm
be patient
be soft
surrender with your heart
change is the explosion of built-up growth
expanding your soul
be gentle
some pieces might have to come apart
to come back whole

I once heard someone say to feel gratitude we must first for-g-i-v-e
hand over our pain
resentment and regrets
to make room for our hearts to truly expand

- the heart needs space —

decisions may not make sense logically
yet still feel right

– our conditioned mind doesn’t always have the best foresight

if you don't shine at all you're dull
but if you spark too much you're unrelatable
and so we try to match the acceptable
dose in which you're alive but not truly living
because if you're too happy others will envy
in a way we are told to follow our dreams but not
really
make sure they stay a hobby
and express yourself but remember others must feel
comfortable around your presence
so when you see someone in the street and you're
having a bad day
rehearse a smile and say you're okay
because it's not normal to have feelings
unless you're in therapy
when we socialize alcohol is a necessity
we must have something to excuse our human need to
be silly
then we wonder why we feel so alone
when we can't stand being the only ones at home
is it because when we look in the mirror we see
ourselves
wearing the layers society has dressed us in?
what if one day we chose to talk off the clothes
the pieces that way down who you are and who I am
the ones that never fit quite right
what if today is the day you let yourself truly be you
and shine as bright as the sunny side?

feel constrained?
tear off the chains
of society
by simply choosing
to live life unapologetically

it's human instinct to fear being rejected
abandoned
we're a species like a wolf
evolved to survive as a pack
it can feel like literal death
to be excluded

when my mind felt polluted
with the darkest thoughts
"should I even be here anymore?"
I was reminded by God
that he is present in every tree

and now I feel his presence in the oxygen
hugging my lungs every time I breathe

faith is the antidote to loneliness

Golden Stars

I rather be judged as I stand naked under the sun
than to hide in the shadows until I'm 95
only to one day look back and think
oh how I wished I was bolder
to choose love joy and the discomfort
even if that meant at others' disapproval

at 95 I'd be wise to know people pleasing is a never-
ending illusion
I wouldn't be scared to be unconventional on a
conventional planet
because what if the ticket out of society is what truly sets
you free?
at 95 I'd know people fear people trusting their souls
it's not logical in the material world
to trust the emotions and wisdom our hearts hold
at 95 I would live life unapologetically
knowing everything on earth is temporary
I'd know we are not responsible for anyone's happiness
but our own
at 95 I would have walked the line and realized there is
no such thing as stepping out of line when the lines were
created by those too scared to step away
so why wait until 95
to live a life you are brave enough today to create?

They wanted her to be good
a good girl

to be fluid like water
to fill up the molds handed to her

they drugged her with praises
when she obeyed

They wanted her to be addicted
to the validation
she never needed

to fear shame
one day
she caught on to the game

kept their pills under her tongue
instead swallowed her power
turned girl into goddess
good into baddest

I stopped asking what they needed to hear and started asking my soul what it wanted to say instead

— *let your soul speak*

a lengthy resume
the perfect grades
extracurricular activities
you deserve to be praised
you've done so well to build up your name

and just like that we're trained to crave
a false sense of validation
employee of the month
the golden child
a blue check mark
but what happens when you're stripped of others' acceptance?
what happens when your praise is replaced with rejection?
you scramble for the mere crumbs of satisfaction
"let me prove to you I am that person you once loved"
they can't see you anymore
they've stamped you with red ink
"not good enough"
they won't give you a second chance to show them who you are
they moved on with life
and now you're expected to too
only it's your choice if you wish to continue to live by their rules
instead shake off the layers that never served you
live unapologetically and own your truth

Golden Stars

let's remember what is real
and by that I mean let's also remember what is not
I don't know when the lines became gray
between real and fake
but I'll lay the blame
in this media world we create
with every post and story we make
painting a picture of a reality that in all honesty
doesn't always reflect the truth
no matter how much we wish or try to
it's a window that you and I can manipulate to filter the light
and let others see what we wish for them to
from the outside
it can seem like the picture is clear
but have you ever reflected on
how content can also be out of context
how relevant does that make social media judgment?
yet we all seem to think we know the full extent of
someone's reality
based on a projected actuality
let's not forget what's real
outside of the sticky web that draws us online
it's the people around us
it's the beautiful complexity of life
it's the time we have away from the screens and how we
choose to spend it
it's our faith our peace and all the emotions that make us human
the real world is multidimensional in so many ways

and like the stars in the sky at night
no digital device can truly ever capture what's in front of our eyes

it’s called a breakdown
because without one
your heart will remain caged
the concrete gates must soften and tumble
mascara stains on your cheeks
it's called a breakdown
because the ice must crack
for the rivers to flow again through the creeks
even though
you may feel broken for a moment
I hope you realize how things break when they expand
like H20 when it’s frozen
so you’re not different
considering you’re made up of mostly water
you’re growing each time you break
I know at this point it feels familiar
to come undone once again

just remember when you ache
it’s just another growing pain

Golden Stars

they say there are 7 stages of grief
and not so differently
there are 5 stages of rejection
the first feels like disbelief
followed by the internal question
"what is wrong with me?"
as your mind scourges to find an answer
you're left alone with the feeling you must be fundamentally flawed
which leads into the next phase of self-hate
even if you don't believe what they say
you can't help but want to crawl out of your human shell
your ego aches
you feel the pain spark up inner flames
which leads to the next stage of rage
anger rooted at the feet of injustice
the only way to exit this phase
is to recognize that you don't need to validate
your worth with someone else's approval
and so you move into acceptance
understanding not everyone will love you
you find comfort in not being everyone's pick on the menu
you can finally remain neutral
this awareness softens your heart
making it easier to breathe
and you begin to see how unaffected you are
by positive or negative remarks
if you make it this far you're led to
the last phase of unconditional love

you love your quirky ways
you love the parts no one claims
you love the ones who don't love you
you love even through the hate

they say don't fight fire with fire
the flames will only grow brighter
don't fight fire with wind
you'll be wasting your breath while the flames spread
don't fight fire with water
no amount will ever suffice the thirst of anger
and in return you will feel drained

and so my friend
if you can't fight fire
learn to dance with the flames
fires are temporary
they will go
how they come
before you know it
they too shall be gone

Golden Stars

Addictions don't leave without
a period of withdrawals
and there's one that has sneaked into society ages ago
it's plagued a big part of the population I would say
it's hard to spot an addiction that's so widespread these days
it's been passed down many generations
it runs in our blood
it's made us all a bit contagious
we spread it with praises and starve it with rejection
this addiction goes by the name of validation
we crave it but like addicts will deny it of course
we'll say we don't care as we pretend not to keep score
of likes on our posts
numbers of followers
we need a daily dose
to keep ourselves from feeling hallow
the only way to break such an
ingrained addition is one of 2 ways
deplete it until you realize you don't really
need it to survive
or consciously let go of the need to feed your ego
it's harder than it sounds to not care
when we've been conditioned to
I suggest we start with the first step
to just simply become self-aware

Alana Lima Johnson

I went back to my hometown
to my old room
I walked through the same back roads
I smelled the same flowers
perfume
I went back to my hometown
looking for a girl I used to know
last time she was here
she was so lost
amongst a group of 20
she felt alone
I found her between the pages
of a diary in her old room
as I read through them
I couldn't help but feel her heart so confused
she would put herself in a platter as
if she was part of a taste tester
validating her worth through every interaction
it felt like a curse
I closed this diary
that one day I called mine
and hugged this girl
wrapping my arms around my own spine
sending love through all my phases
I've been through over time
I'm not the same girl
I once used to be
I hope that girl feels saved by me

Golden Stars

I used to buy more clothes to seal the gaps in my closet
like how I picked up extra work to fill my hours
spoke too much to avoid the silence
always ate so I felt full
or at least I tried to
fill up a space in my chest with everything but the necessary
with all the things but nothing at all
a void that like a black hole felt infinite inside
and I thought maybe if I lied to myself
and said I had everything and more I'd believe it
truth and self-love are the only things that I needed

if someone judges you
for choosing the things that bring you a smile
for taking the leap on your wild dreams
for trying new things
send them love
for the only reason someone would judge
Is because they haven't given
themselves the chance
to follow their own soul urge

my hair still kisses my cheeks the same way as before
the left side of my lips still curls when I smile
and I'm still the kind to stop on the side of the road
to wave the cows hello
but yet I am now someone you no longer know
I hold my gaze longer if I'm being confronted
I don't let their words penetrate my skin
and although I'm still soft I lift up my own chin
I'm still the same person when I look in the mirror
but nothing inside feels familiar
I've grown through the mud
held my own heart through each growing pain
and when I was re-birthed
I finally recognized my strength

it takes strength to be soft
it's easy to build walls around your heart
numb your healing scars
project instead of love
the catch is that
you must have the courage
to feel the pain
in order to truly feel anything once again

when it comes to feeling
you don't get to choose
you have to feel it all
allow life to be your muse

the duality
thc contrast
the array of emotions
is not for the weak
your feet may feel sore
as you walk through this thing we call life
but my love
don't allow your sore feet to
be the reason you no longer dance
with the moon at night

I don’t want to end up stuck in between grief and regret
I want to live a life I’ll fear to one day forget
I don’t want to grieve a person
I wish I had the courage to become
I don’t want to regret the moments
I never created when I was young

art is often rejected by critics
and see
you are art
a masterpiece painted with strokes of human complexity
not every eye can appreciate or understand
your beauty
in a white room on display
you may be too much for some people to take in
or the perfect piece for someone's home
but like art you'll be perceived differently by everyone
even rejected by some
and so all there is left for you
is to embrace the duality of perception
and remind yourself
you are art
and art doesn't strive for perfection

I don't know when I'll see my last golden sunset
hear my favorite country song one final time
lay in bed with my lover
as the moonlight invades the privacy of our window pane
I remind myself of this when my heart feels bitter
when I resent the ones I love
when I take time to forgive
every day we are dying and this is not how I wish to live
so I made a promise
I'd let go more easily
loosen the grasp of my pride
when I'm feeling upset
I'll be the first to apologize
so we can turn bitter moments sweeter
and cherish the finite nectar of life

Golden Stars

we don’t rush sunsets
we wish time would slow down for a moment
as the sun unforgivingly sinks into the horizon
yet we don’t feel such an attachment to the sun when it’s noon
assuming we have so much of it left to consume
but if time is just a construct
and a day of sun represents our eternity
ending at a sunset
wouldn’t you want to grasp
all the moments in between when it rises and it sets?

the only way to rise
back from the past
is to drop the weighted belt you wear
the one that carries your anger and regrets
all the words you wish you said
the only way to surface
is to alchemize the darkness
and swim up towards the light
the only way forward
is to leave behind
what no longer serves a purpose
be the lotus

it's in our nature to try to compartmentalize
make sense of life's chaos
give reason to our actions
but what happens when intuition
feels so strong yet there is no logic to back it?
because the heart is wiser than the mind
and it tends to be a feeling of steps ahead
will you follow the lead of your beating chest?

the thing about intuition is that it will not always make sense
it's not meant to
so you must decide if to question its wisdom or leap at its guidance
neither will seem like a seamless path
to question means to forever wonder
to leap may cause your whole world to shift before you
the thing about intuition is that
it's a short-term guest
it's a sudden whisper
that can feel like a massive punch
then it's gone
it won't reason with you
it won't try to convince or sway
it defies logic
and begs you to make a choice
will you go or will you stay?

they say people grow bitter

I think they mean it in the same way weeds take over an
abandoned garden of flowers

in the overpowering way a single thought can taint a
whole day

but bitterness
is a choice

and you can't be bitter
if you choose forgiveness.

— *you can choose to make life taste a little sweeter*

if I could do it all again
I would beg life to starve my ego
so I could learn to feed my heart and soul
from the very start

isn't it a bit contradicting?
that the things in life that require the most strength beg of you to soften
letting go of people who have sailed off this world
releasing those who have come into our life for only a fraction of time?
release is an exhale
your muscles including your jaw must relax
to embody that strength you must be soft
and surrender when the future's secrets weigh on your mind
yet you must allow your spirit to take flight into
the obscurity of the unknown
of what's yet to come
surrender is like falling asleep
you must loosen the grasp
on the need to control
again you must soften
to have strength is often mistaken
as climbing a mountain

but rather it's taking the leap from the top
and having the courage to trust all odds
even the ones that may very not be in your favor
knowing that regardless of it all
you can remain like salt water in freezing weather

Golden Stars

I was once told “you can hate what they did and still love them”
and that’s how I wish to approach anyone who’s done me wrong
recognizing their soul for its purity in existence
separating them from their actions
honoring their spiritual magnificence
giving myself permission
to find love in my heart
regardless of the hurt they may have caused

the greatest test of love
is not to love when it's easy
but to love when it's hard
when you realize the only way
forward is to love through the unjust
the unkind
the anger
to love through the regret and the resentment
yet there is no way to love without dissolution
of what was once on its way
the walls must tumble
and so love must be greater
so overwhelming that it swallows
any emotion less than
you may wonder
how it's possible
to love the very thing that may stir hate
you may beg the world to give you a reason to love
yet sometimes silence is the answer
you must love as it is
as it was
as it will be
with no control over how things will unfold
and so
you must love with no expectation
you must love selflessly
love masked as forgiveness
forgiving when there is no apology
forgiving when there is pain

forgiving when you are right
that is the biggest test of love
to open your heart and let go
when the world gives you every reason
not to
open your heart and see love
in the darkest room
and recognize you are able to see love past it all
because at the end of the day
the love that you see
is a reflection of your ability to
love even when it's hard

I was a lost ship caught in a hurricane
my sails ripped while navigating the storm
I had no idea how I'd arrive back to shore
so I closed my eyes and prayed to god

he showed up as a lighthouse
guiding me back home
he whispered with the wind
and told me to not fear the rain
it was all part of him
and so I followed his light
and when I arrived
I had a little more understanding
of life with him by my side

Golden Stars

I craved your golden star stickers
but you gave me gray circles instead

until I blended in with the
gloomy skies on a rainy day

you labeled me and I let you
my tears bled your words

I lived amongst the charcoal clouds
it felt like a curse
until one day every sticker you ever gave me shed off my skin

this only happened when I prayed to God
he told me to look within

when I surrendered to the love that lived in my heart
every gray circle effortlessly fell off

but the biggest miracle is I no longer cared for gray circles
and even less for your golden star

Alana Lima Johnson

my hands ache from grasping so strongly
to the threads of my life
the parts I can't control
that have been weaved and stitched without my permission
into my experience
I try to pull them apart
to rearrange
and yet I am reminded once again
I am not in charge of crafting this life of mine
I sometimes get to choose
the fabric and colors I like
it's fun and makes me linger for the desire to control
every piece that's sowed
but whenever I grasp too strongly
I bleed as I get in between the needles
my scars they sting
and I once again am humbled
I finally chose to let go of the need to be in control
instead I open my heart
and choose to witness the beauty of a great master
performing his art

“do you believe in god?”
he asked me as tears clung
onto my chin “what?”
I replied
caught off guard by his soul-intrusive eyes

“ I do but I don’t think I know him
if that makes any sense”
he smiled and let out a friendly sigh
“you should talk to him then”

he noticed I was confused
so he continued
“all this pain
the emotions you feel
at the end of the day
are all material
they’re illusions
like vivid dreams
if you talk to god more he’ll show you
what’s behind life’s movie like scenes
this veil that brings you to your knees will fade
and as you soften your grip
your eyes will adjust to a new level of clarity
you’ll finally see and also feel the most seen”

— *have you tried talking to god?*

if you find yourself constrained by life
your heart wrapped within its vines

you'll notice the more you fight
the harder it will feel to breathe
you'll feel practically paralyzed

breaking free from its grasp
is having the strength to be soft
allow yourself to melt off like butter

think - unclenching your jaw

detaching from this world
noticing this human costume you wear is
merely a piece of clothe

the journey through death and birth
is like cycling through your wardrobe
there is no such thing as "good or bad"
and so you can choose to remain neutral through it all

one of people's biggest regrets before they die
is living a life by someone else's guidelines
sometimes that simply looks like
not doing a 180 in life
if it's what feels right

what do you do when the unknown calls you?
summoning your name into a forest of potentiality?
there is no moon tonight
a sheet of darkness covers the sky
yet the wind whispers into my ear
go ahead
it's your time
sometimes you need to go
find the fire that burns in your soul
light up a match
sometimes in order to grow
you need to dive into the vast unknown
I promised myself
maybe a week or a lifetime ago
that I would lead my own way when the winds called my name
that I wouldn't stay and watch my fire grow cold
it was my time
I had already known
so with cold fingers and trembling hands
I light up my torch
there is something familiar about this place
I can only describe it as a warm embrace
hard to explain
a poetic dance
a solo journey
while at the same time
we hold thousands of hands

there's something magical about dawn
when light kisses darkness
hues of blues and oranges
a reflection of how beautiful it is
to alchemize our own shadows in life

Alana Lima Johnson

looking outside my window
I see the sun kissing the mountaintops
birds gently gliding through the valley and a rainbow
fading into the vastness of the sky
I sit there with a book and a cup of lavender tea in my
hands
the next day I'm back at my window pane
except the view doesn't look the same
the mountains are covered by lead-gray clouds
lighting veins like roots
summoning the rain and thunder
I sit there and ponder
on how beautiful both views are
the contrast between the light and the dark
that encompass of the same sky
doesn't differ too much from our own duality inside

Golden Stars

I rather be an honest chaos and feel alive
than live a life where I have to lie
to my soul every day that one day I will listen
one day I will choose me

I rather live a life where I feel the rollercoaster of
emotion
than a life where I've numbed myself to the point
where my smiles are rehearsed

I want to be alive
I want to test how far I can expand until my soul is
sore and collapses amongst the
hands of the universe

I want to be so alive that when you
look me in the eyes on my final days
you don't see a fading gaze but rather a heart that was
once wise

I sent every person that hurt me *love*
because holding on to the pain
was drinking poison from a cup
I was happier sober
so I no longer needed that drug

behind closed doors there is another world
behind a smile could be a broken heart
you only know your own *narnia*
in someone else's closet there could be webs and thorns
yet we humans have become actors
some of us the best of our kind
using smiles and laughter as covers
ashamed of our own demons and scars
social media is the ultimate setting
for enhancing the perfection of an imperfect life
in some odd way
connecting online also makes us feel further apart
in a world of humans with battle wounds
that are blind to the eye
we believe we are the only ones scared

Alana Lima Johnson

I used to think homes were built with four walls
colored concrete and wood floors
I used to think homes were found with people
settling or traveling abroad
I was wrong
these homes don't withstand every storm
home is found within the flesh and bones that hold us upright
the blood and the heart keeping us warm at night
like turtles we've always carried our home on our spine
when we realize we can be our own shelter
no one
no hurricane
can ever make us feel homeless again

there is a duality in emotions we often don't speak of
the way a sunset brings peace and maybe a little bit of
sadness when it leaves
the times we are usually our bravest are also when we
feel the most fear
the way birthdays are full of love and maybe some tears
there is a complexity to how we feel in each moment
because the highs remind us of the lows
and at the lows we are grateful for the highs
you can grieve and celebrate life when someone passes
it's confusing at times to assimilate what we feel
it's ok to feel it all
it's what makes our emotions vulnerable and real

it takes courage to walk away
because anytime we step forward
we leave a version of ourselves behind
permanent shadows like imprints
so we may always remember
what are where we came from
too often we are scared to detach
from who we are
because doing so if followed by
the inevitable question
“who am I now?”
may the beauty of life be the quest that we can’t
quite ever figure that out
for we are much greater than what
words can describe
so my love takes the leap
and allows the new you to shine

Golden Stars

we fill empty drawers
we break moments of silence
with random remarks

thoughts clutter every second of the mind
we avoid the void
at all times

there's an uneasy feeling
of empty space
empty inbox
empty house
emptiness
a hollowness
that craves to be whole
and so we fill them with anything
place holders
puzzle pieces that don't belong
we force their corners to fit the holes in our life
how we will force relationships
despite it not feeling right
the gaps must always be closed
and then we wonder
why we're so claustrophobic
we beg for space
yet we don't allow it
what if we did allow people to go
and not be replaced?
what if we stopped avoiding
the void in the first place?

if you are hurting
create art
sometimes
it's the only way
to alchemize
pain into something beautiful

remember
the only people criticizing people making art
are the ones too scared to pick up the paintbrush

your experiences may pave roads that lead to scars
and the inevitable trails of broken hearts

confessions pressed between pages of a half-written journals
trying to make sense of why things
had to end

not too long ago
it felt like life finally made sense

and in the middle of the undoing and
the mending back together
of your heart
you start to wonder
if you are deserving of people made up of
run-on sentences
instead of periods or question marks

I just hope that regardless
of what you've been through
you always remember your worth doesn't diminish

when the sun sets
the footsteps
are also washed
from the shore

your experiences don't define your self-worth.

Golden Stars

I met an old woman at a grocery store
her body was sore from living
in her eyes she held more than 10000 stories
not all of them she wished to remember
but I couldn't help but feel her tender heart
and admire it for remaining soft
she told me she lost her son
her cat was sick
and her husband had left her for another
yet she smiled and laughed about the times she sneaked into
2 movies at once
traveled to her hometown
and skinny-dipped for the 50th time on
the same lake by the local playground
her heart had 100 reasons to be bitter and hard
but she cultivated forgiveness
and even though it was still scared
it didn't shut off or discard the beauty
and the polaroid memories she carried from life
and at that moment
I made a promise
to always find a reason to soften
when life gives you 100 reasons to harden

chaos has taught me
the only way to dance with peace
is to embrace neutrality

Golden Stars

I no longer waste my time forcing things to happen
I let things be easy
I let people meet me halfway
I let projects take their own turn
I let it happen
and I let myself find gratitude in the outcomes I cannot control
what a peaceful way of living
to just allow things in and out of my life with ease

there's only time for love and loving
there's only time for forgiveness and softening
when you look back at all the years you lived
when a lifetime feels like a moment
you'll wish you spent your time
writing poems
dancing at 2 am
calling old friends
and making amends

Golden Stars

everything changed
when I decided to start noticing
the yellows instead of grays
how the sun rays
in the morning turned my white walls golden
how my favorite mug was painted with sunflowers
how turmeric made
every meal a little brighter
it’s funny how things change when you
start noticing yellows instead of grays

you can try to mute my thunder
however energy that is suppressed only
grows louder

you’re so strong
for remaining soft
your heart permeable
like volcano rocks
even after everything you’ve been through
you’re here hosting friendships and lovers and family
in the living room of your chest
you’ve renovated this space
taken down every wall
that may once have been in place
you don’t walk like you’re broken
you walk like you’re whole
but only the ones who know

it takes strength to open
when everything within you says “don’t”

she freed herself when she realized
she had nothing to prove

Golden Stars

I live my life in prayer now
and that looks differently every day
but the one thing that always remains
the same is the way I choose to open my heart
to the things I can't understand with my brain
like how to forgive someone who has no regret
how to love through the pain
how to accept the things I can't control
I realized in the heart the word "how"
is nowhere to be found
and so I leave it open
to love without logical reason
to love myself
everyone
and life
through every season

I'm immune to your thoughts
to your words
to your perception of me
now don't get it wrong
there's only one way to build immunity
I was once beaten to the ground
by the same things that no longer
trigger me now
only after feeling the pain
I rose through the ashes of my old self
and learned to love my soul
this love of mine built a shell
a pearly white shield
protecting me from your words
and just like that through love
my immunity rose from the dust

what's the lesson in your pain?
every ache holds wisdom

there's eternal knowledge
running through your veins

choosing to be honest with myself
triggered
the collapse of the hollow castle I had built

and at the end
I have you left to thank
I used to see you
as the source of my pain
to a certain extent
I still do
but I wouldn't have grown
without the challenge you put me through
truly I wouldn't trade that growth for months of peace
I'd choose the turmoil the anger and grief again and again
if it means I can stand
a little stronger on my 2 feet
so here I am saying thanks to you
for being the rough waters
that made me even more grateful
for the peaceful seas

it's an honor to be each other's mirror
and at the same time one of the most
challenging things we can do for one another
the weight of an honest reflection
can feel like a lot to carry for someone
if they are not ready to see their own
truth in the glass before them
they'll see through it
and meet with your face
the anger will rise
and you'll be the one to blame
every pain reflected back at them
is suddenly projected at you
and if you're not conscious of it
you'll start to believe their accusations are true
and reflective in nature
there's no such thing as putting the mirror down
even if you are to leave
it'll be the same thing
when you meet someone
next time around
and so the only thing there's left for us
to do is to remind ourselves that we are just reflections
and someone's perception has actually
nothing to do with you

how do you choose yourself after years of self-neglect?

when the standard has been set
that you are the waterfall to everyone's desert
there is bound to be a rebellion
when you redirect
the flow of your love
to nurture your own flowers

I watched as two so-called enemies met death at the same time
they swore to never cross paths again
yet their roads were tied to the same vine
and after life's unwavering twists and turns
they reached the end of the stem and there
they both were standing on the edge of no return
scared and reflective
knowing time never stops and it wouldn't stop now
the tickling of the clock
the days running up
and as they both reflect on everything that life encompasses
laying on the same hospital bed a few hallways away
in the midst of their own pain they had
empathy for the person in whose
name they dared not say for years and silently
as tears filled and blurred their fading gaze
they prayed that the other would also find relief
some kind of peace in the end
if they could go back and change one thing
it would be to never have spent
time resenting another person
because as they're about to go
as the tension in
their hearts melt

so does their pride and ego
and they see that
even their worst
so-called enemy
was just a soul like them
also trying their best
to solve life's greatest quests

I pray for my heart to be more like butter
enriching the lives of others
but too slippery to grip anything too tightly

— detached

your self-worth is not something you can
measure
prove or
earn

let me be shameless like nature
not shy to create or release

let me be shameless like love
brave to fall and crack open

let me be shameless in the way which
I twirl through the world with faith

freed from the constraints
of worrying about
“what they would say”

it's all material
these big feelings
these complex relationships
these life situations
be a witness but remain detached
for all of it
like a cloud in the sky
should also pass

you don’t need golden stars
when your soul beams brighter than
the sun
even on the days that feel like nights

but if you ever need to be
reminded of your eternal glow
remember you’re much more than
these flesh and bones

you’re a spark within your human vessel
a flash caught in a bottle

light seeping through a linen sheet
you’re golden
much brighter than
the human eye could ever see

Acknowledgments

To my family and friends, thank you for the unconditional love and support through all of life's phases.

God, thank you for guiding me back to my heart and helping me see through this material experience.

Love,
Alana

Note from the author:

After following my heart and intuition and making some very bold, life-altering decisions in the name of love and choosing myself, I exposed myself to what I didn't know I wasn't ready for—people's opinions, judgments, rejections, and rumors.

I desperately tried to explain my decision and my truth, yet no one seemed to see or hear me.

This painful experience led me to go inward. The only way to make sense of any of it was to write. And slowly, I started to realize that the problem wasn't them; it was me.

I needed to feel accepted. I wanted to be liked and loved. I was the one tormenting myself.

After digging even deeper, I came to the realization that I, like many others, was conditioned to crave external approval. This took me all the way back to the golden star sticker days many of us are familiar with as kids: the desire to please someone to get just one more golden star and the excruciating pain of having a star ripped away when we don't do or act as desired.

With this awareness, the layers of this false need started to melt away as I wrote. In its place, unconditional love for self and others bloomed, and so did my connection to God.

I hope these poems hold you through the process of softening and finding the freedom to let go of the need to fit in, to make sense to others, or to be anything but YOU.

Love,
Alana Lima Johnson

www.ingramcontent.com/pod-product-compliance
Lightning Source LLC
LaVergne TN
LVHW010606160826
845677LV00013B/3283

* 9 7 9 8 8 9 3 7 2 3 7 2 4 *